The Nature Kid's Guide to
WHALES

RENATA MARIE

LP Media Inc. Publishing
Text copyright © 2023 by LP Media Inc.
All rights reserved.

For information address LP Media Inc. Publishing,
3178 253rd Ave. NW, Isanti, MN 55040
www.lpmedia.org

Publication Data

Whales
The Nature Kid's Guide to Whales — First edition.

Summary: "Learn all about Whales, the Nature Kid Way"
— Provided by publisher.

ISBN: 978-1-954288-72-0

[1. Whales - Non-Fiction] I. Title.

Title: The Nature Kid's Guide to Whales

CONTENTS

ACROSS
THE SEA

Sploosh! **A Humpback whale leaps from the ocean.**

Whales live all over the ocean. These giants travel from sea to sea. **They swim under cold ice.** They leap near sunny shores. They search for food. They sing to each other.

There are about 90 types of whales. The ocean is so big. People are still discovering new types of whales.

GIANTS
OF THE
OCEAN

A big animal swims in the deep blue. It's a Blue whale!

Blue whales are the largest animals on Earth. They can be over 100 feet (30 meters) long. They can weigh over 300,000 pounds (136,078 kilograms).

Whales can also be small. The Dwarf sperm whale is only nine feet (2.7 m) long. It only weighs up to 600 pounds (272 kg).

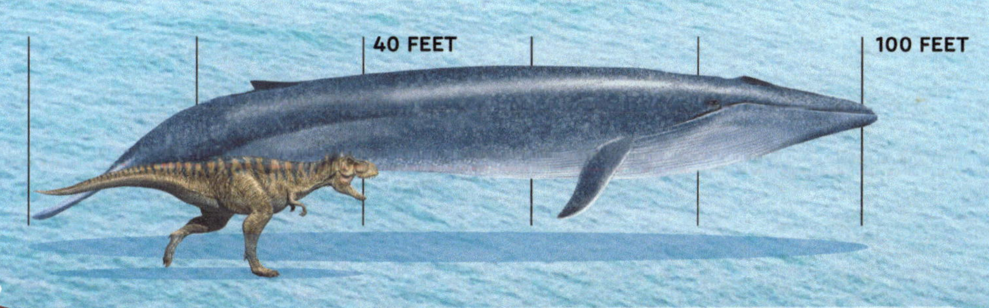

Blue whales are the biggest animals to ever live on Earth. They are even bigger than dinosaurs.

SEA
MAMMALS

Air shoots out of the water. A Fin whale takes a breath.

Whales are **mammals**. They breathe air through blowholes. They can hold their breath for up to 90 minutes. **They are warm-blooded.** They have hair on their heads. They use their heads to feel what is around them. They give birth to live baby whales. They feed them milk.

Whales, dolphins, and porpoises belong to the same family. Killer whales have the word "whale" in their name, but they are actually dolphins.

SUPER SWIMMERS
FUN FACT!
Fin whales are the fastest whales on Earth. They can swim up to 23 miles (37 kilometers) per hour.

A Southern Right whale sails through the water.

Whales are powerful swimmers. Their tails are called flukes. They move their flukes up and down. They push the whales forward.

Their long bodies slip through the water. **They use their fins to change directions.** They look for food and open their mouths wide.

Whales come in two groups. They can be Toothed Whales or Baleen Whales.

Toothed Whale  **Baleen Whale**

DINNER
IN THE DARK

Click ... Click ... **A Sperm whale searches for food.**

Toothed whales dive deep to find food. Sperm whales can dive 10,000 feet (3,048 m) deep. It is dark in the deep sea. But whales can use sounds to find food.

Toothed whales use echolocation. A whale will let out a click. The sound hits an animal and comes back.

The sound tells the whale where the animal is swimming. It tells the whale how big it is. It even tells the whale what shape the animal is. Then, the hunt is on!

Sperm whales are the largest toothed whales.

DEEP SEA BATTLES

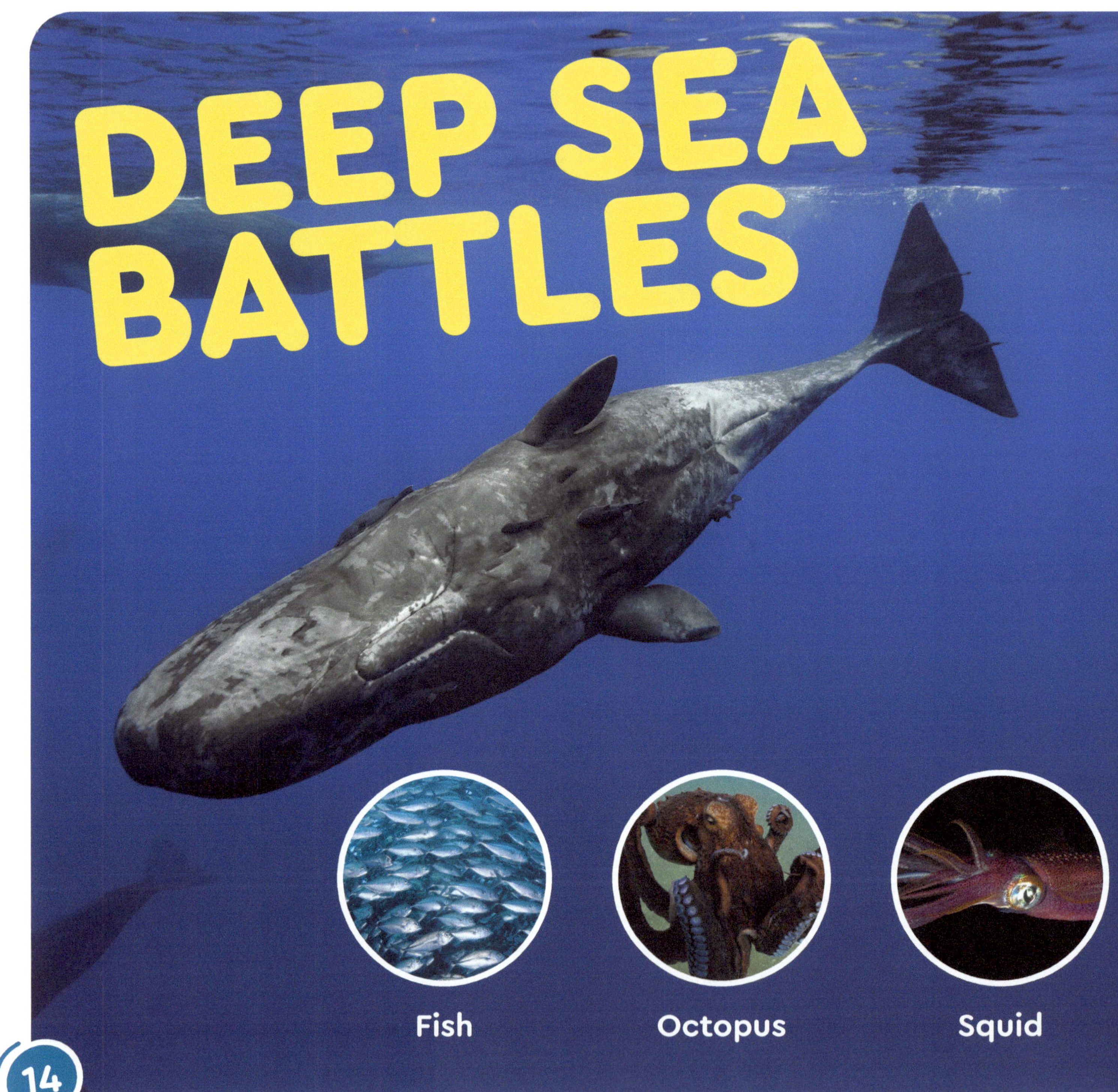

Fish

Octopus

Squid

A Sperm whale dives towards the deep. He's hunting for Giant squid.

Toothed whales eat squid, fish, and octopuses. Sperm whales suck their prey into their mouths and hold it there with their sharp teeth. **But squid fight back.**

Squid can be 60 feet (18 m) long. Their arms are covered in sharp suckers. They seize the heads of the sperm whales and hold on.

Sperm whales often leave fights with full stomachs and cuts on their heads.

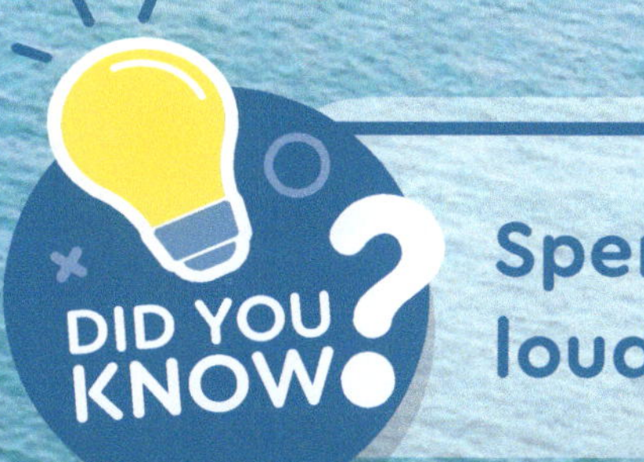

BIG
MOUTHS

Fish race away from the giant mouth of a Bryde's whale.

Baleen whales have baleen instead of teeth. Baleen is long and thin. It lets water out and keeps prey in.

Baleen whales eat small fish, krill, and plankton. **They swim slowly with their mouths open.** They take in big mouthfuls of water. They push the water out of their mouths. It flows between the baleen.

Animals cannot fit between the baleen. They are trapped and become lunch.

Baleen are made of the same matter as fingernails and hair.

BUBBLE NETS

Pop. Pop. Pop. **Fish jump in a circle of bubbles.**

Humpback whales circle a school of fish. They blow bubbles. **The bubbles form a net.** They push the fish together. The fish swim to the top of the water and the whales charge.

Their giant mouths break the surface. Folds from their throats to their stomachs open. Their mouths hold more water and more prey.

Full, the giants sink back under the waves.

FUN FACT!

Whales jump from the water. Their splashes are loud. They send messages to faraway whales.

WHITE
WHALES

A white whale swims through the icy Arctic. It's a Beluga whale!

Belugas live in the Arctic. The water is cold. But whales stay warm.

Whales have **blubber**. **Blubber is fat.** It keeps whales warm in icy water. It gives them energy when they cannot find food.

In the fall, ice spreads across the Arctic. Belugas swim south.

Belugas have squishy foreheads called melons. Their melons change shape when they make sounds.

JUST KEEP SWIMMING

A Gray whale swims across seas. She has a long way to go.

Gray whales swim the farthest of all whales. In the spring, they swim north. The cold waters are full of prey. **Their blubber keeps them warm.** But baby whales are not born with a lot of blubber.

In the fall, gray whales swim south. They give birth to baby whales where it is warm and safer from dangers.

Gray whales can swim up to 14,000 miles (22,531 km) each year. That's over halfway around the Earth!

BIG BABIES,

A big baby Humpback whale swims beside her mother.

Baby whales are called calves. Blue whale calves are the biggest babies on Earth. They can be 23 feet (7.0 m) long. They can weigh 6,000 pounds (2,722 kg).

Calves drink their mothers' milk. **They swim next to their mothers.** Their mothers push most of the water away. The calves swim easily and they stay safe.

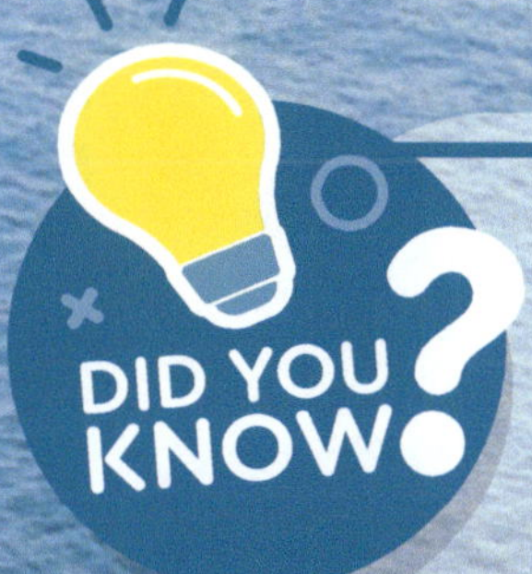

Blue whale calves drink up to 150 gallons (568 liters) of milk a day.

TAIL SLAPS

False Killer
Whales

Great White
Sharks

Killer Whales

A young whale races behind his mother. Danger is near.

Adult whales are usually too big for predators to take down. But calves are small. **Killer whales, false killer whales, and large sharks hunt whale calves.** But mother whales fight back.

They put their big bodies between the predators and their babies. They slap their strong tails. They make loud sounds.

When attacked, Sperm whales form a circle. They put their heads in and their tails out. They keep their young safe in the center.

FRIENDLY
FLIPPERS

Up, down, and around. A group of Sperm whales swims together.

Some whales live in groups. A group of whales is called a **pod**.

Toothed whales are friendly. They usually live in larger pods. **Smaller whales need a pod to stay safe from predators.**

But larger whales are too big for most animals to attack. Baleen whales live in small pods or swim alone.

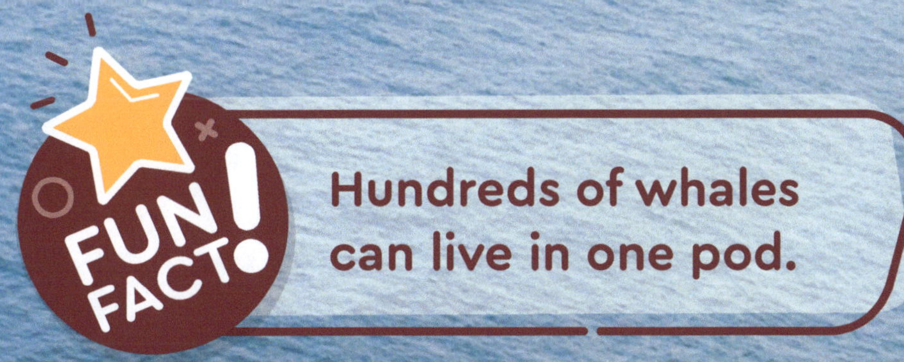

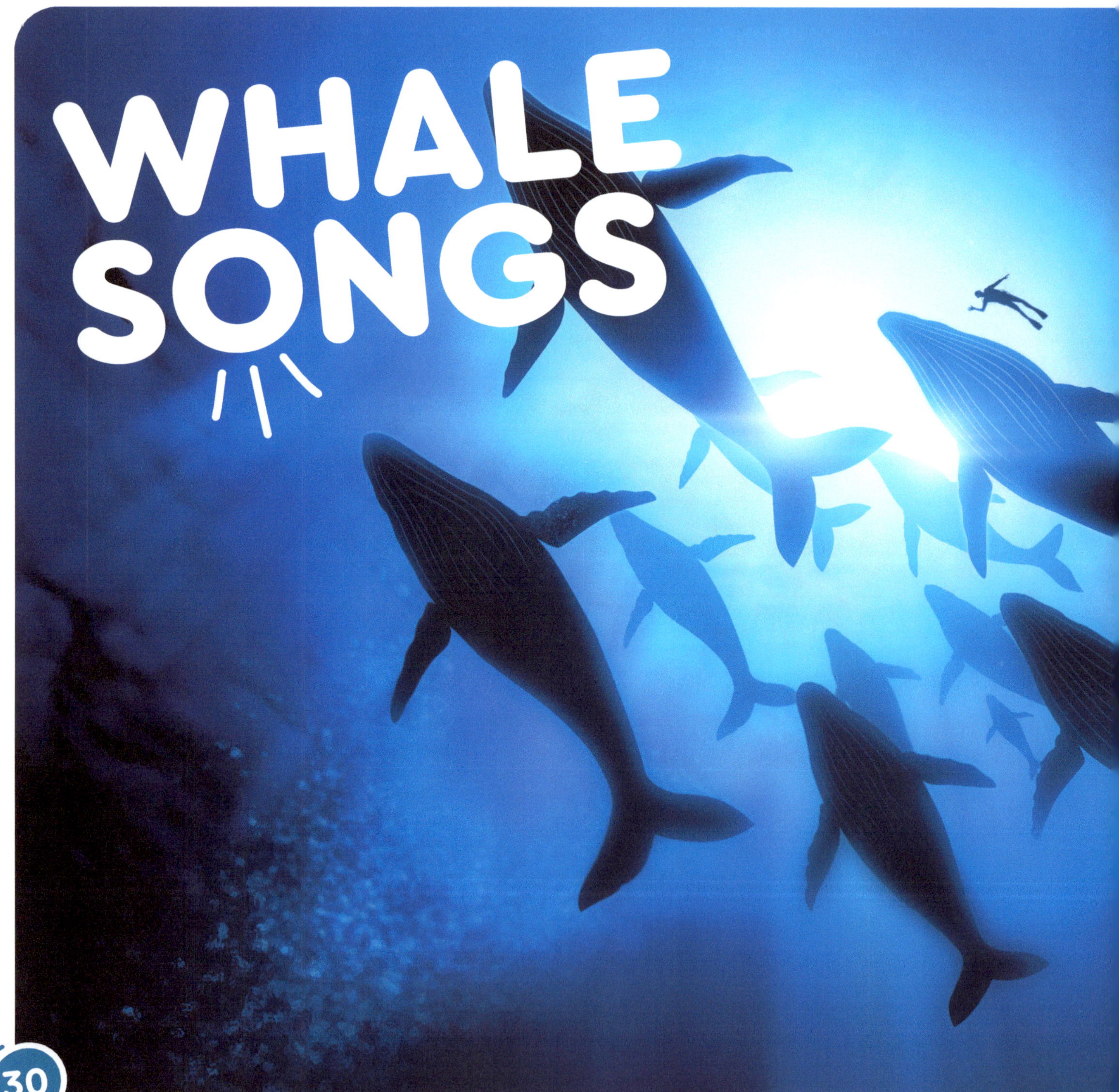

WHALE
SONGS

Whale songs fill the sea with music.

Whales sing to each other. Baleen whales make low sounds. Toothed whales make clicks and **whistles**.

Each pod has a different song. Whales learn songs from each other. Their songs change over time.

Males sing to find females to make calves with.

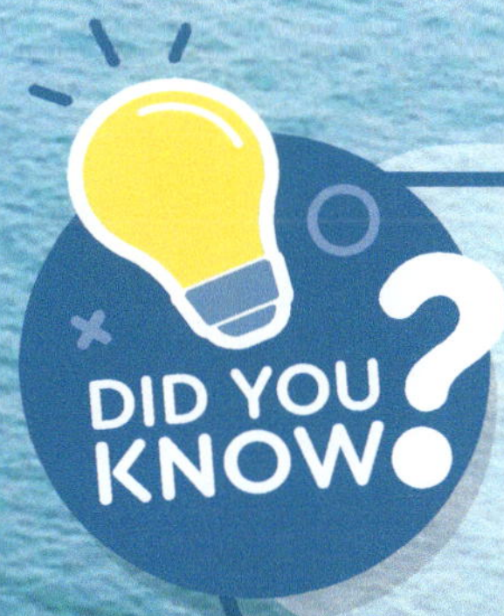

Most whales stay with their mothers for about one year. Some stay even longer.

EXTRA LONG TOOTH

DID YOU KNOW?

Only male Narwhals have a tusk. Females almost never do.

A horn rises out of the water, it's a Narwhal pod!

Narwahls live in icy waters near the Arctic. Some people call them the unicorns of the seas because of the long horn that sticks straight out of their head. **But it is not a horn, it's a tusk.**

Narwhals use their **tusk** to sense the world around them and find food in the dark and icy waters.

Narwhals dive deep to find their food, sometimes going down hundreds of meters to feed on squid and fish.

PLAYFUL OCEAN JUMPERS

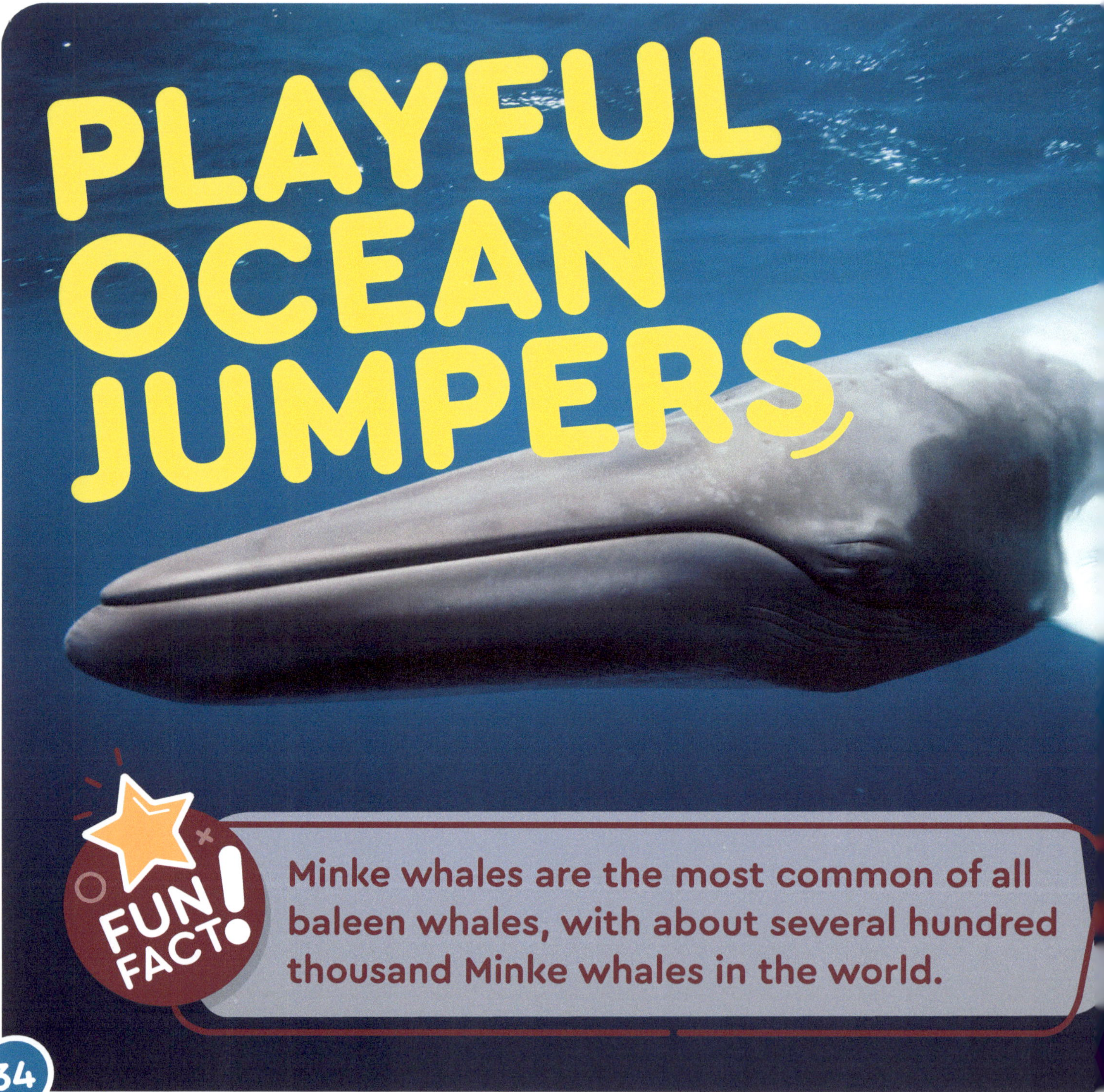

FUN FACT!

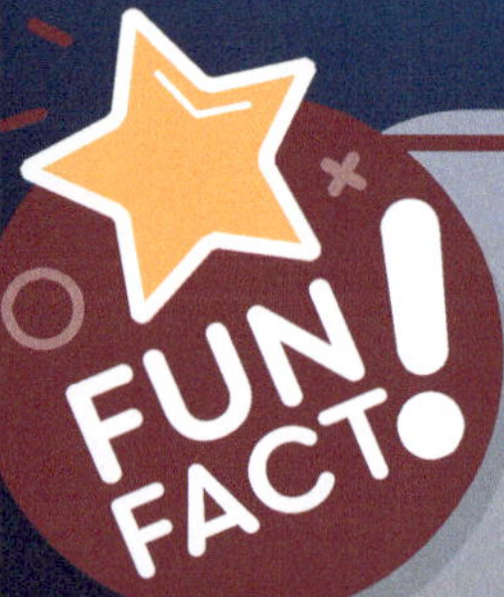

Minke whales are the most common of all baleen whales, with about several hundred thousand Minke whales in the world.

A small whale quietly swims up next to a boat. It's a Minke whale!

Minke whales are one of the smallest types of baleen whales. They are found in oceans all over the world. They are known for their playful jumps!

Minke whales are very curious. They often swim up to boats.

They are easy to spot because of their colors. They have a white band on each flipper. They have a white area near their throat.

UNSAFE
SEAS

**A whale swims and swims.
But no matter where she goes,
humans are nearby.**

Whales across the world are dying out. They swim into oil spills. They swallow plastic. They cannot hear each other's songs. **They are hit by boats.** They are tangled in nets. They are hunted by humans. They are losing their homes.

Whales were almost hunted to death. People wanted their bones and baleen. They wanted their oil and meat. Now, it is illegal to hunt whales in most countries. But some people still do.

BIG BLUE

A net is cut. A whale swims free.

People want to help whales. They cut whales from nets. **They clean plastic from the ocean.** They built a tool to tell ships when whales might be in the area. They are trying to make less noise in the water. They hope whales can have a healthy, safe home and swim freely in the big blue sea.

If a whale is on a beach, do not put it back in the water. It could be sick or hurt. If it is in the ocean, keep water out of its blowhole. Put water and wet towels on the whale. Keep people away. Too many people will cause stress. Call wildlife helpers.

GLOSSARY

blubber
a thick layer of fat

pod
a group of whales

echolocation
using sound
to find things

tusk
a long twisted tooth

mammals
animals that feed
their babies milk.
Humans are mammals

whistles
to make a
high sound

MORE AMAZING ANIMAL BOOKS from Nature Kids Publishing!

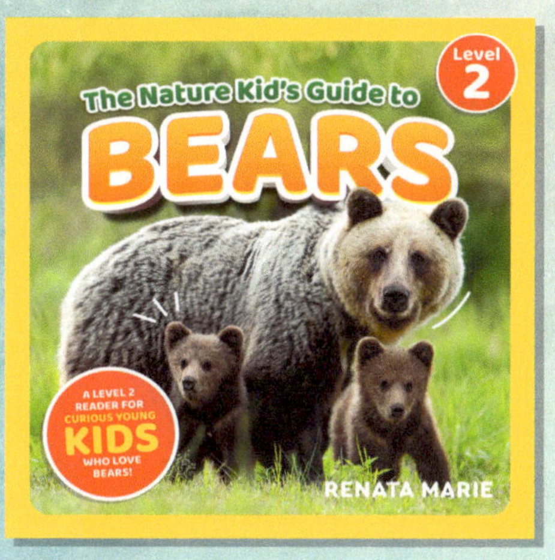

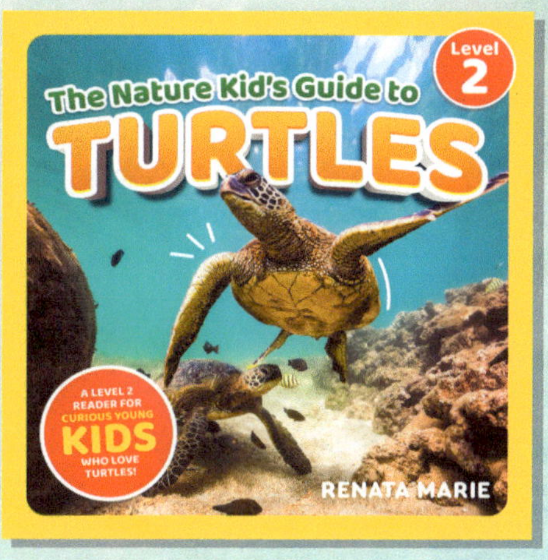

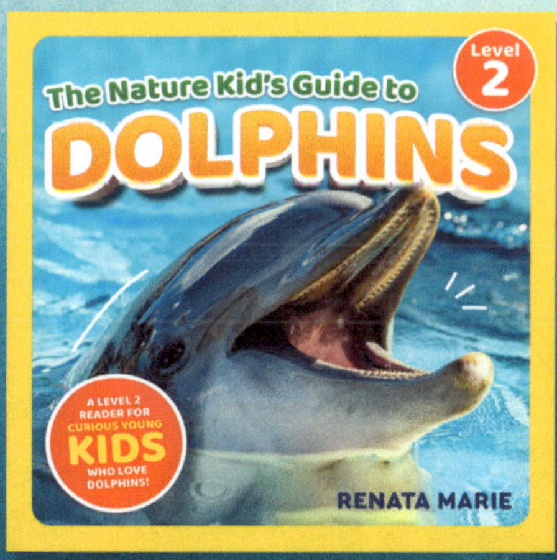

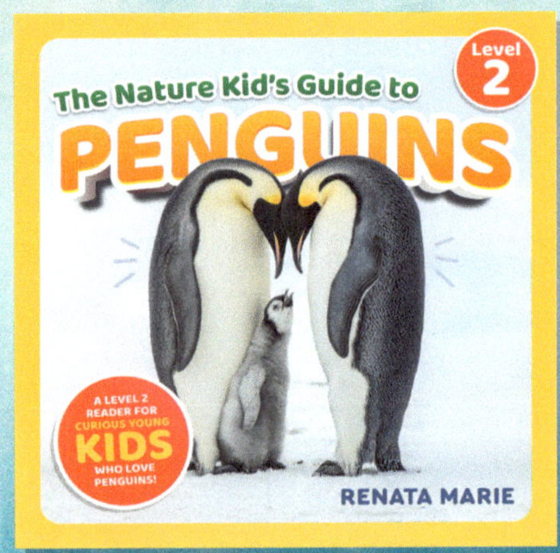

Visit NatureKidsPublishing.com to Learn More!

www.ingramcontent.com/pod-product-compliance
Lightning Source LLC
Chambersburg PA
CBHW042123030726

47599CB00002B/330